PENCIL STROKES
An Affirmation Coloring Book

Written and Illustrated by
R. Heather Ropes

2021
IRIS RENOVATIONS, LLC

Author's Note

Please enjoy adding your glorious colors to the coloring pages. On the back of each you will find its related thought-provoking essay. Enjoy creative coloring, positive pondering, and affirmative fun!

Blessings,
R. Heather Ropes

ISBN: 978-1-952911-23-1

Front cover image by R. Heather Ropes
Cover design by Victorine Lieske
Book preparation by Prairie Muse Books Inc.

I look carefully, finding the beauty, joy, and hidden blessings in my day.

STEINBECK IN FLOWERS

I look carefully, finding the beauty, joy, and hidden blessings in my day.

Have you passed by gardens and people whipping through your daily tasks without actually noticing much at all? Do you really see the individuals within a group? We might not take the time to appreciate the brilliant color of a flower or notice the height of its stalk, but wouldn't it be nicer if we did? Wouldn't it be more satisfying to really connect with a person rather than generally acknowledging them just as part of a group?

It takes intention to manage life and let beauty enter each day. I hope you will take a moment to touch flowers. Greet the person you are near. Appreciate brilliant colors and really give your attention when you pet the dog. We all need those beautiful moments where we can appreciate a hidden blessing. I hope you find yours.

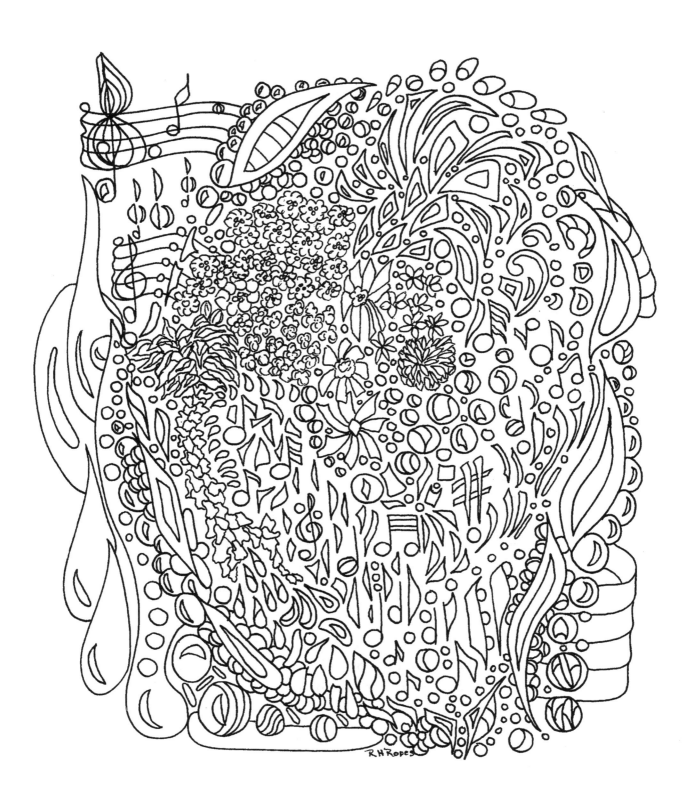

*Today I dance, knowing I am a note in a chord
in a song of universal composition.*

Musical Explosion

Today I dance, knowing I am a note in a chord
in a song of universal composition.

My first love, Cooper, opened a recording studio in Tennessee after his touring days with bands. His contribution to the lives of songwriters, musicians, listeners, and dancers will live on in the memories of thousands. Music is the common language of Earth. It can instantly create the backdrop as memories flood in.

I'll date myself, but some of my favorites are my great-aunt Marfie singing along with Nat King Cole in the kitchen at the ranch. Mom jitterbugging to songs on the juke box in Maryland. I remember learning "America the Beautiful" from Mrs. Peterson, my third grade teacher. Jethro Tull songs remind many Denver metro kids of being tear-gassed at Red Rocks amphitheater on June 10, 1971. Don't forget those romantic songs like "Unchained Melody" and many more sung by Alicia Keys, Harry Connick, Jr., Garth Brooks, the Kingston Trio, and of course, Etta James singing "At Last." Hearing songs from childhood, school days, or a memorable event can instantly send our minds back in time or cement the here and now in our memory banks.

Wouldn't it be lovely if governments played parts in a unified world symphony to which we could all sing and dance? Many musicians do unite the world. Beethoven, Bon Jovi, and the Beatles have done a great job of spreading melodies throughout.

Be brave. Go ahead. Dance and sing. Know that you are a critical note that harmonizes in a chord echoing throughout our world!

My shelter is in harmony with the earth. I am secure and rest within.

Adobe Home

My shelter is in harmony with the earth. I am secure and rest within.

I had the privilege of living in a genuine adobe home in Albuquerque. In Taos, New Mexico, I learned how to make walls of an Earthship home by pounding dirt into old tires. These two construction styles provide exceptional harmonious, earth-friendly shelter.

Mankind has changed the surface of Earth by drawing on rocks and digging deep gouges for mineral resources. Dammed rivers have wiped away ecosystems and human communities to provide hydroelectricity for multitudes or irrigation for desert golf courses. Sometimes concerned groups have reversed damage from past "improvements" by planting trees or by ratifying eco-friendly laws. Modern societies use massive amounts of natural resources. I like my electric hairdryer, but I've recycled and used cloth shopping bags for more than 30 years.

Homes are created in McMansions, towering skyscrapers of condos, suburban cookie cutters, one-hundred-year-old rehabs, or tiny houses. No matter your choice of style or size, I hope you incorporate elements that support harmony with our Mother Earth. Rest securely and well.

Like water falling into a tranquil pond, I allow Spirit to flow through and around me.

WATERFALL AND POND

Like water falling into a tranquil pond, I allow Spirit to flow through and around me.

On the occasions when I get near falling water, I find it easy to just sit and be.
I am observing nature's metaphor for receiving the never-ending God Source.
Where is your place where you pause and feel the flow of the Higher Power?
Envision the place where you feel connected to the Universal Good, God, the
Spiritual Source. If you don't already have a piece of artwork that takes you
there, I hope you will use this drawing, and your color choices, as reminders
to accept and receive that which abundantly flows to us all. Allow it all in.

Grateful for the air, I breathe deeply, acknowledging the Law of Circulation.

THREE TREES

Grateful for the air, I breathe deeply, acknowledging the Law of Circulation.

Next to a Nebraska lake, I pondered these tress and their gift of circulating air elements. Having taught students the circulatory nature of electricity, life cycles as they relate to predators and prey, and gas exchange in plants, this scene reminded me of the Universal Law of Circulation. Many religions and cultures of the world teach a form of the basic tenet that it is good to give and to receive.

I think giving and receiving manifests greater heart space. Blessing another with something that is no longer useful to you creates physical space for that which is a better fit for your current circumstances. Knowing the item will help another feels good. The Law of Circulation is cyclical movement that increases good on several levels. Step into the cycle and consciously circulate in some way today. Bless another and you will be blessed.

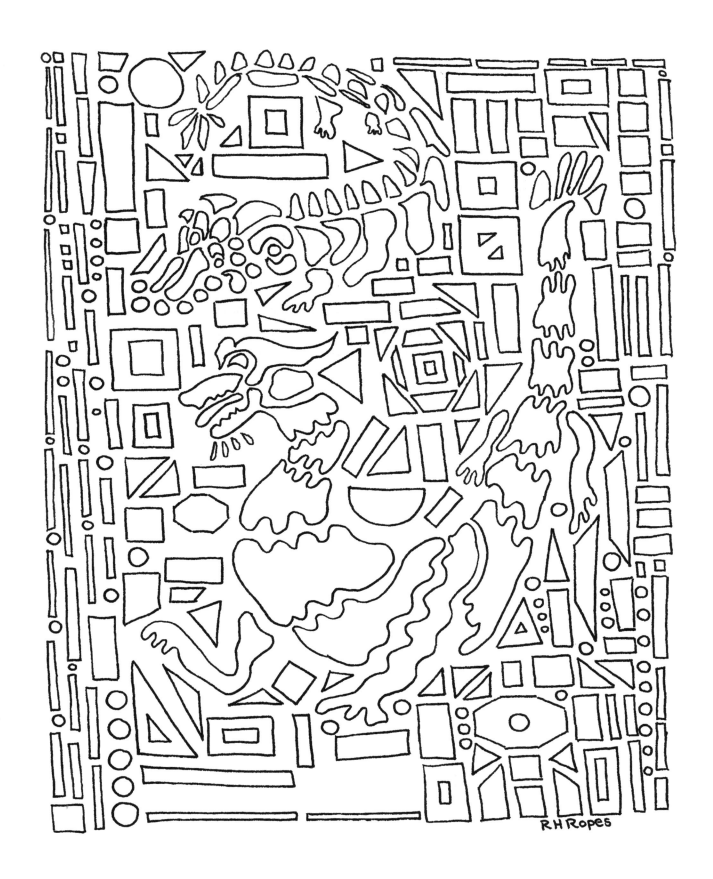

I move, march, and dance through the streets expecting good fortune.

Dragons

I move, march, and dance through the streets expecting good fortune.

Asian celebrations often include beneficial dragons. The expectation of benevolence, strength, and good luck from the dragon has moved beyond Asian borders. Good luck charms, images, and blessings are received with joy. When you walk today, imagine the dragon boat gliding by, dragon kite and tail soaring above, or the meters long colorful dragons parading beside you. Expect good luck and strength being gifted to you!

Nature's music and poetry lift my mood and increase my contemplation of joy.

Wildflowers in the Rockies

Nature's music and poetry lift my mood and increase my contemplation of joy.

Music may be retrieved through recording. Poetry may be words read from a page. However, when I look out and see a valley full of wildflowers against a background of snow-capped mountains, I see poetry of the earth and feel music in my soul. It is too rare when I stop my schedule to give myself the joy of quiet beauty. Whether observing a sidewalk planter or majestic panorama, take some time to listen to the music and poetry of the land today. Contemplate joy!

I push through. I reach up. I unfurl to drink in and receive my full blessing.

UNFURLING FERNS

I push through. I reach up. I unfurl to drink in and receive my full blessing.

Ferns amaze me. Their dormant crown sits above or just below the earth
through the frigid winter. In the spring, the delicate-looking spirals push
clods of dirt out of the way as they reach for the light. Growing daily,
suddenly a delicate profusion of fronds are decorating the length of my home.
No matter what you are pushing through at this time, reach. Even if fragile,
I believe you too will fully unfold for a blessing.

To some, I am unusual. I freely express my talents, gifts, contributions, and my place in our diverse world. I am needed and loved just as I am.

FANCIFUL DIVERSITY

To some, I am unusual. I freely express my talents, gifts, contributions,
and my place in our diverse world. I am needed and loved just as I am.

I loved Dr. Suess books when I was a kid. Okay, I still do.
His ability to create fanciful creatures brings such joy
to people all over the world.

Sometimes my pen just needs to do a fanciful dance
on paper. Express your fancy self today!
There is no other you.

I have faith that, given time, my struggles lead to beauty.

Bursting Iris

I have faith that, given time, my struggles lead to beauty.

There is a miraculous plan that is innately coded into each flower. The compact forms grow around one another until petals take their turns unfolding, revealing incredible veined beauty. Like the iris, I will choose to know in the core of my being that my struggles are leading me to a beautiful result. Even if you or I don't understand yet, let us have faith. We are growing. We are maturing gloriously. We will see a beautiful result.

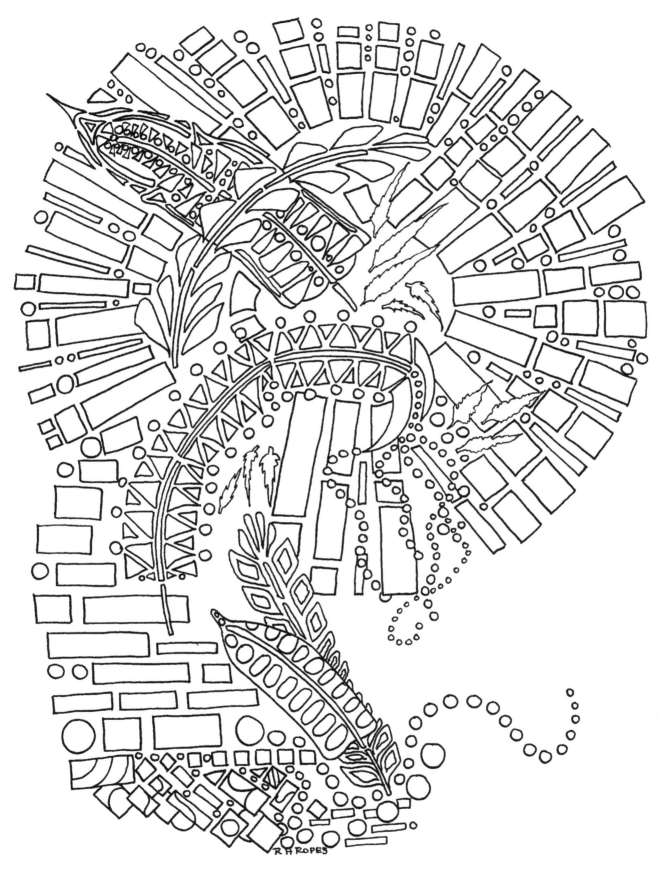

Birds need rest for migration. I give myself time to rejuvinate
along my life's journey, too.

FEATHER JOURNEY

Birds need rest for migration. I give myself time to rejuvinate along my life's journey, too.

Witnessing the migration of Sandhill Cranes brings people from all over the world to Nebraska in the chilly spring. These birds with six-foot wingspans have flown from Mexico and rest to gather food along the Platte River before continuing to Alaska. 600,000 birds migrating anywhere from 170 to 450 miles a day need their fuel! They need their rest, also.

What is the population of your bustling community? Is there a 24/7 busyness? Are there times when it rests? Europeans are much more likely to rest and vacation than Americans. All humans need rest and relaxation. Have you forgotten? Are you giving yourself the rejuvenation you need?
Are you refueling? Take a break during your journey. It's okay.

Minds grow the fruit of thoughts. I choose positive seeds for my mind.

GIRL WITH FRUITFUL MIND

Minds grow the fruit of thoughts. I choose positive seeds for my mind.

Right-minded thinking. Vision boards. Affirmative statements taped to mirrors and dashboards. Songs with uplifting lyrics. Having the faith of a mustard seed. All of these reminders help us focus on positive aspects of life. During challenging times, the ancient science and practice of thought-directed energy can help us react in a more positive way than we might otherwise. Give yourself the fertilizer you need to grow positive fruit in your mind. Plant positive seeds.

I celebrate imagination and delightfully play along.

Fairy Tea Party

I celebrate imagination and delightfully play along.

Do you remember making pirate hats from huge rhubarb leaves? Outlining walls of your fort with pinecones under a tree? Having a tea party with teddy bears or dollies? The imagination of children needs to be nurtured. Electronics constantly feeding our children images is changing their brain chemistry and ability to imagine.

Think of all the colors you are choosing. Imagine them, sharpen up, and delightfully create! Can you help a child unplug and engage with their imagination or offer support to an organization that does? Every child needs the ability to create a fairy tea party or a friendship fort.

I am a positive link in today's chain of events.

LINKS

I am a positive link in today's chain of events.

As I go through my day, I want to be a positive influence. My gift in the day may be greeting my faithful postal worker, smiling at a stranger walking past me, or doing my job really well so the next person down the line doesn't have to correct errors. In a myriad of ways these encounters are small links in a chain of events.

Just like the paper chains created in classrooms, go out and be a link in someone else's chain. Have fun!

I remind myself to search and learn about those
beyond my immediate surroundings.

BIRD AND FIELD

I remind myself to search and learn about those
beyond my immediate surroundings.

In this drawing, I envisioned the bird being able to fly, but needing the reminder to leave the safety of the home tree and expand its horizons. We can all get comfortable in our neighborhoods, so much so that we might not even venture to other parts of our own city. Sometimes I need to remind myself to get out of the safety zone and explore.

I would love to have a big travel budget adding experiences and stamps to passport pages. I know I can virtually travel via the Internet and learn about other places viewing PBS programs. But it just isn't the same as having the personal experience.

I have been fortunate enough to explore Hong Kong and Kowloon. With the comfort of being able to speak English there, I was able to explore an entirely different culture. I also have lived in another country long enough to modestly communicate in their language, enjoy their food and festivals. The greatest reason for looking beyond our own fences however, I think was best said by Mark Twain and often quoted by Rick Steves. "Travel is fatal to bigotry and narrow-mindedness."

May you venture beyond your boundaries. Plan an experience! So much is gained when flying from the nest!

Remembering those who have stood bravely for betterment, I too shall do my best to make this day better for someone else. An act of kindness has power!

FLOWER POWER

Remembering those who have stood bravely for betterment,
I too shall do my best to make this day better for someone else.
An act of kindness has power!

I began drawing this flower type in the age of flower power. The simple design was meant to symbolize peace. Television show set decorations to Marimekko fabrics from Finland used this hippie insignia. The 1960's wasn't a peaceful time. Some of us remember protestors putting flowers in the ends of rifles held by incredibly young soldiers. Some of us cried because of low military draft numbers our friends had drawn. From a lot of diverse viewpoints, protests, sadness, compromise, and loss of leaders, the 1960's did usher in legislation that was meant to make a more level playing field for all Americans. The struggle continues. It takes the efforts of so many to make a better world.

So far, it doesn't seem to be my mission to be a grand influencer like Eleanor Roosevelt who opened the skies to the Tuskegee airmen; or Edith and Grace Abbott, fierce advocates with nationwide impact regarding child labor, immigration, and social justice; or Susan La Flesche Picotte, the first Native American woman to become a physician. My power nurtures others on a much smaller scale. Do small efforts matter?

I have fed a hungry neighborhood kid. It mattered to her. I have used my work, voice, and vote to improve education. It mattered. I volunteer for Habitat for Humanity's ReStore. It matters to the employees I help and the customers I assist. I have a welcoming garden from which many can eat. I create art and affirmations for higher good. I believe the little things we all do can add up to create a more empowered beautiful world.

So, what is your flower power? I know you contribute. I know you believe in affirming the positive because you are interacting with this book. Color these flowers with the joy that you bring to others through your efforts, no matter how small! Color them kind! Color them powerful!

I am one of many who contribute to the greater vision of our community.

POPPIES

I am one of many who contribute to the greater vision of our community.

Me. You and me. We. Us. Did a picture in your mind expand when reading those words? Who is the other that makes 'you' an 'us'? Who is in your group that is the "we" in your mind? Humans have so many categories into which we can fit. For example, students can belong to different schools with different mascots. Competition can be divisive or good-natured within and between local communities. However, when the Olympics comes around, whole nations cheer for an athlete without concern for which school they attended, or state they came from. Nothing smaller than the national collective matters. With national colors waving, not even their sport matters! The power of focused optimism and pride can impact even the very last person over the finish line.

From an inclusive viewpoint, educators, suppliers, retailers, service personnel, fixers, doers, givers, and recipients appear as a fluid group with a common geographical denominator. These parts are nurturing each other and the community as a whole.

Your community is the symbiotic reflection of a healthy garden – from seed to dropping petals of full maturity. Leaves circulate gases. Roots and stems circulate water and nutrients. Petals give beauty. Pistils and stamens help repopulate. You are one of many. Today, be the one who holds the affirmative mindset of visualizing each in your community serving and meeting the needs of all. You are powerful!

Comparing myself to another is like asking the chrysanthemum to be a pothos.
I am the only inevitable aggregate of my human and spiritual being.

Mums and Pothos

Comparing myself to another is like asking the chrysanthemum to be a pothos. I am the only inevitable aggregate of my human and spiritual being.

Insecure as the new girl at school, I observed the popular girls and did my level best to be like them. It didn't work well. Years later in my dorm room, I made a list of attributes I admired in other women. My work to incorporate those ideals led me to become a better, stronger me; no longer the wishful imitator.

We too often are told by media influences to admire the early bloomer, the taller and prettier, the rounder, the thinner, the California girl, the athlete, the New York City Wall Street magnate. Instead, I want to shout out, "Be that which you are!"

God didn't make a mistake creating you. From your cellular structure to your interests and talents, you are perfect for the being you were meant to be. Now I'm the creative woman who wears color combinations that my sisters say only I can pull off. Light fixtures, wall color combinations all reflect me. "I couldn't live with this, Heather, but it works!" I beg you to take this in. If you are the chrysanthemum, bloom fully! If you are the pothos with variegated leaves, grow to great lengths! Dowse yourself in the miraculous fertilizer of your spiritual practice and human experience as only you can!

I plant seeds of imaginative possibilities knowing harvest is near.

Fairy Cottage Farm

I plant seeds of imaginative possibilities knowing harvest is near.

When I was very young, I would share stories of the fairy people who lived in the Bozeman, Montana, house we shared with our relatives, the Kolstads. Thankfully, my great-grandmother never discounted or disputed my interactions with my little friends. Remarkably, no one in my family discounted my multiple planes of existence.

In the attic bedroom at the Kolstad ranch near the Canadian border, there were stacks of Disney comic books from the 1940's. Inside very special ones little bug communities repurposed a myriad of small human items. A matchbox became a bed. Thimbles became buckets. Empty spools of thread became tables. I was fascinated and would re-read the illustrations even more closely than the dialog.

Here is one little friend's home for you to color that I harvested from my memory. Enjoy planting your imaginative seeds of possibilities.
What will you harvest?

Because little ones are watching me, I am my best self.

Role Model Bird

Because little ones are watching me, I am my best self.

The smallest of observers are such great mockingbirds! There may be so much going on around, below and above them and yet, there they are mimicking their elders. I used to try to be just like my cousin, Chris Kolstad, a mere 12 years older than my four-year-old self. I'd mimic his walk as best I could. Later I would do my best to be cool. Then, as a mother, I had to really watch myself! Finally, as a teacher, I was on display.

More and more teachers are expected to model and teach children good manners, how to react, share, and in general, be good people. Some children come to school lacking so many basic life skills and needs that it can be overwhelming. I have worked with so many fine teachers and para educators who are very consciously working to be their best selves each day in order to teach subject matter and people skills. If you can, please find a way to contribute to the education of little ones by supporting teachers. If you call your local school, I bet the administrative assistant knows of a need. (They know everything.) Your gift of any support will be appreciated!
You will be showing your best self, too.

Today is an opportunity to be kind, to love, to grow,
and to appreciate my health.

KINDNESS, GROWTH, HEALTH

Today is an opportunity to be kind, to love, to grow,
and to appreciate my health.

Drawn before the days of Covid 19, but being published during the pandemic, the emphasis on being kind to one another and appreciating good health is foremost in the minds of the world's populations.

In my neighborhood, we unselfishly render acts of kindness. We ebb and flow with these acts. No one is keeping count. Together we give from our hearts and grow in spirit. Counting butterflies with little ones in the garden or shoveling snow for an elder, watching birds or baby raccoons together, all are opportunities to circulate kindness. Imagine if each day, each human gave at least one act of kindness to another being or the earth. My dad is very limited in physical capability, but he can almost always make another person laugh.

Be grateful for all that you are able to do, no matter your level of health.
Take care of your body lovingly and opportunities to use it
to be kind and grow.

*Like a fine quilt, I consciously create the background
to complement each of my goals.*

FLOWER QUILT

Like a fine quilt, I consciously create the background
to complement each of my goals.

This simplistic flower quilt design begs for background. I held myself back from filling it in for two reasons. First, I thought you might like to share coloring time with someone who is more comfortable with a more simplistic design. The other reason is because my dear friend Lisa, a talented quilter, prefers muted tones and designs while I like bold colors with intricate patterns. This page begs you to have fun designing your block backgrounds. Solids. Circles. Stripes. Blended colors. What will you choose?

My son Griffin and Lisa's son Sean played hockey together. Our lives have been stitched together ever since. In fact, I remember Lisa first learning to quilt. It began with a borrowed sewing machine and hockey T-shirts. Now she owns a humdinger machine and creates masterpieces, even a Mona Lisa quilt! She has reached such creative goals. Piecing together blocks to create a quilt is like piecing together the building blocks necessary to accomplish goals. May you have beauty while reaching your goals.

Cycles of days, months, seasons, and years contain moments I remember with joy.

CYCLE OF JOY

Cycles of days, months, seasons, and years contain moments I remember with joy.

Life is made up of circles and cycles.

Circles. Circular bubbles. Bubbles forming with an infant's gurgles. Children chasing bubbles. Newlyweds walking through bubbles. Hope bubbles up. Then bubbles burst. Circles of friends, co-workers, families. Prayer circles. The circle of life.

Cycles. Gatherings to celebrate annual celebrations, births, birthdays, holidays, unions, reunions. Seasonal colors surround you as we cycle through the year. Spearmint. Fuchsia. Marigold. Tomato. Prairie sky. Umber. Crimson. Pumpkin. Evergreen. Holly berry red. Crystal white. The life cycle.

I hope coloring this cycle will ignite your memories of truly joyful moments.

*I have set my keystone in place. As a unique expression of Spirit,
I give thanks and walk through my archway of expectation.*

STONE ARCHWAY

I have set my keystone in place. As a unique expression of Spirit,
I give thanks and walk through my archway of expectation.

Fluctuations in faith happen to most of us. At times I have felt confident with school, career, family, and travel experiences. These were the building blocks for my life. Other times I've had my life shattered, feeling like the keystone crashed down upon me as I stood under the archway. During the earthquake of my life, others held me up with their positive thoughts, prayers, and many helpful actions. With gratitude and renewed strength gained from their invaluable aid, I had to chart a new course. A new keystone was carved, lifted and installed.

May you also have those who know and believe in your strengths and help support your archway during tremors. Now, with your keystone in place, walk through the archway with a sense of purpose and expectation.
Express yourself fully!

Travel enlightens and informs me. I joyfully plan a journey.

JAPANESE GARDEN

Travel enlightens and informs me. I joyfully plan a journey.

From a very early age I have loved to travel. I moved from Georgia to Virginia, Maryland, and then Montana by age four. Beginning at age fourteen, I'd save my babysitting money and buy student stand-by airline tickets. People, places, food, art, architecture, and culture have delighted me my whole life.

As a Navy family, we worked hard to educate ourselves so as not to offend while experiencing different parts of the world. Sometimes we got the information right. Sometimes we didn't.

Trevis became fluent in German. Griffin could correct people on their facts while waiting in line to enter a castle or museum. Me, well, I packed a great plaid dress and matching shoes as my nice outfit for the Ballet Folklorico and museum day in Mexico City. Let's just say in Mexico my wearing red shoes didn't translate to, "I'm a mom completing my Spanish language requirement." I had some interesting conversations!

An airplane ticket isn't necessary to have authentic cultural experiences. A hometown restaurant row may open doors to many different cultures. In Lincoln, Nebraska, one can eat honest-to-goodness African, Vietnamese, Indian, Mexican, Greek, Tai, and American foods. Plants and settings from around the world can be found in many formal city gardens. Take someone's hand and depart the neighborhood for a cultural journey. What stories will you have to tell? Check your shoes.

It is a sensational day for dancing with intuition and imagination!

HAPPY DANCING FLOWERS

It is a sensational day for dancing with intuition and imagination!

I couldn't help myself when drawing these flowers. They just make me smile and want to do a happy dance. I imagined the flowers all red. Then blue. Then mixed colors that blend toward a vibrant center. When I color this page, it shall be with intuition and imagination leading the way. Please use this page as an invitation for your mind and body to do the same.

Dancing with intuition and imagination is natural for children. They play changing from one activity to the next without regard to the 'have to' and 'should' adult world. Want to play like a child but with the advantage of having transportation and snack money?

If you could have one great day, imagine with whom, what or where you would play. Take a step and plan at least this first element of your sensational day. Next, simply follow your intuition from that starting point to see where your guides, angels, or gut feelings take you. In the evening, check in with yourself. Did you do a happy dance? Was it surprising and colorful?
I certainly hope it was a freeing opportunity full of discovery.

I burst forth from my firm foundation. My inner light reflects my true purpose.

Light Bursting Forth

I burst forth from my firm foundation. My inner light reflects my true purpose.

I hesitate in divulging my circuitous route of spiritual learning because I do not want to offend, but if not for the spiral of exposure and questioning that continuously lifted me up to a greater understanding, I would not have become me. So, I am sharing this with a tinge of fear and a brave foot forward.

My foundation has been built with the help of many. I give thanks for the sermons of Rev. Dr. Terry Cole-Whittaker and Pastor Ryan Kelly, the writings of Ernest Holmes and Unity's Daily Word, Penney Peirce, Louise Hay, and many more. I also built upon my understanding in Women's Bible studies with Debbie and Annette, meditation and prayer groups and from my Lakota teacher, Anne. The direct communication with God, Jesus, and the messengers that I believe have been sent to help me, whether in my fourth grade Vacation Bible School in Corvallis, Oregon or being in nature in different parts of the world, I have felt the knowing truth I am a child of God, the Universal Infinite Intelligence, who watches over me and connects with me, even in the retched portions of my life.

I believe that no matter how stable or rocky a person's past may have been, we have been given the power to choose, the grace and the forgiveness that will enable us to create a new direction for our lives. It takes determination, work, and faith to restack fallen blocks, carve new ones and stack them even higher.

I learned how to reach out, affirm my thoughts and direct my energy to build a more stable foundation and a greater connection to the Infinite Power. If you want to build anew or add to your current foundation, do so. Shine!

Love grows in me, moves through me, and is reflected back to me.

LOVE GROWS

Love grows in me, moves through me, and is reflected back to me.

A wild plant has the freedom to reach in any direction. Runners spreading. Seeds flying. New blossoms sprouting hither and yon. Plants intertwining with others in the field. While many don't or aren't allowed to feel it, there is a wildness in most human lives, too. Rarely does a human have a straight trajectory for their life or the ability to predict where and when love connections are made. Like the untamed, love has a way of intersecting with the runners in our lives. Hopefully, most of us have experienced the positive aspects of love best described in Greek terms.

- Agape – the selfless love of all. Mother Theresa comes to mind.

- Philia – a love or deep comradery within a tight-knit group such as military friends. Navy wives have this down.

- Storge – the natural love between parents and children or family members. I'd certainly include my aunts, uncles and grandparents.

- Ludus – puppy love or playful affection. Oh, the teen years!

- Eros – a sexual, can't get enough of you, love. Did you end up marrying this person?

- Pragma – the long, patient love evolving over time. My grandparents epitomized pragma.

- Philautia – the spectrum of this word runs between narcissism and feeling secure with compassion for yourself. I've known some and I'm working on the later.

Color the wild runners of love varietals! May you have them all in your life!

How boring if all birds were similarly feathered.
I relish the finery in my diverse flock!

Bold Feathers

How boring if all birds were similarly feathered.
I relish the finery in my diverse flock!

My stepmother's love of birds and her collection of found feathers reflect different colors and patterns among species. Scientists and students who study nature gain an understanding of the function and beauty of diversity. The ecosystems of forests, jungles, deserts, oceans, valleys, and mountains, thrive because of diverse yet interconnected flora and fauna. The different ecosystems of the world work together to nurture the entire planet.

The positive side of human cultural diversity can either be viewed as differing aspects with beauty to share and an opportunity to expand understanding, or negatively, racism and the 'them versus us' mentality. The world is suffering from extremism as I write. Racism. Poverty. Divisiveness. My hope is that more of us can appreciate the beauty of people in our communities who have infinitesimal differences in DNA, but might feather their nests a little differently.

Our grandparents may not have approved of tie-dye shirts, low-cut bell bottoms, long hair, marriage outside of religious or racial boundaries, but chances are loved their grandkids anyway. Tattoos, sagging pants, and bright green hair are not my choices for finery either, but I try hard to get over it and realize these are just another form of feathers.

Can we remember to take the opportunity to be open before closing our minds? Yes. Let's function together at a higher level and focus on the finery of diversity.

I acknowledge the divinity of each of my cells. I accept their perfect replacement power, purpose, and growth pattern. From my cellular level outward, I exude joy.

JOYFUL CHRYSANTHEMUMS

I acknowledge the divinity of each of my cells. I accept their
perfect replacement power, purpose, and growth pattern.
From my cellular level outward, I exude joy.

Give children real microscopes. Direct them in dissection. Guide them so
they can make their own slides and watch the joy erupt around the room!
Enthusiastically, they see the beauty and difference in cells from various parts
of the flower body. They appreciate each other's work and realize
they are real scientists.

Just like the flowers, our bodies are glorious works of divine planning. I invite
you to appreciate the highly differentiated cells in your organs, muscles,
bones, and systems. Invite their mastery to fill you with a joyful appreciation
of interconnected wholeness. See them as they truly exist (as in under a
microscope) or imagine dancing ovarian cells in pink tutus and eye cells as
rolling circles with halos, all giving you the gift of magnificent healthy joy!
Even if parts of you are missing or bionic, know you are divinely whole!
Today, exude joy from deep within your cellular level outward
where all can see.

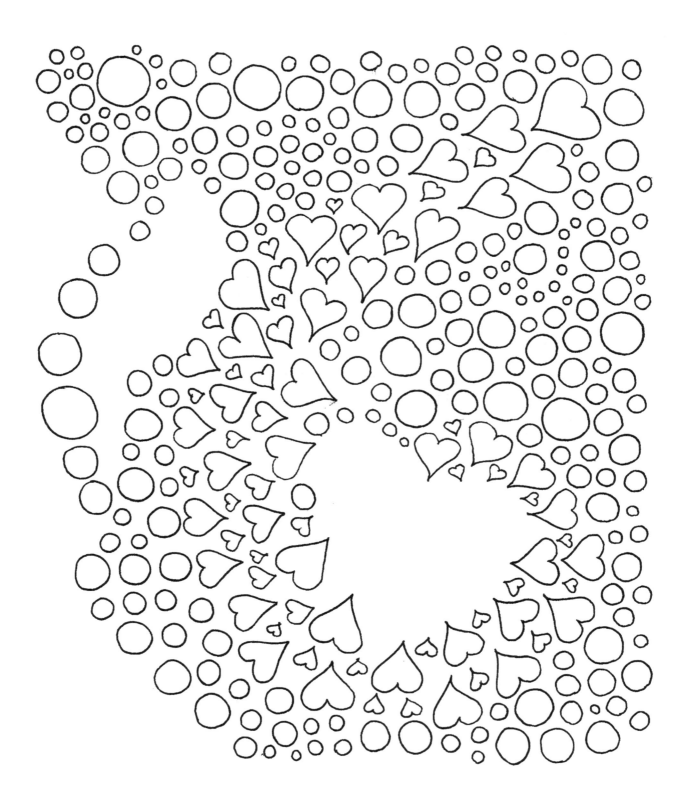

An effervescence of love bubbles up in me today!

Effervescent Hearts

An effervescence of love bubbles up in me today!

I have given bubbles instead of candy during classroom Halloween parties. The cookies and candy were left on desks and the joy of chasing the bubbles and blowing the most or biggest replaced the sweets. Some bubbles connected, showed rainbows, elongated, released rapidly or grew slowly with great care.

Like bubbles, some people lovingly connect to us for short moments in time. Pop! They are gone. Like a big bunch of bubbles, we see the many faceted sides and shifting rainbows in others linked to us for longer periods. Luckily, some bubbles, like dear loved ones, last a very long time. Our admiration and love for them is so enormous we think we'll burst.

Let love bubble up simply by remembering those whom you care about deeply. Chase and touch some love today!

I choose to bravely let my voice be heard by leaders.
A profusion of good can come from my voice and views.

POTTED PLANT PROFUSION

I choose to bravely let my voice be heard by leaders.
A profusion of good can come from my voice and views.

I once taught for a school district whose Board of Directors did not exemplify good leadership. They voted 100 times over several evenings with the same deadlocked results, just to choose who would run the meetings!

Exasperated, I wrote my comments down and took my turn to address this governing group. Nervously, but eloquently then forcefully, I told them there isn't a teacher today that doesn't help their students learn how to negotiate, compromise, and come to consensus in order for the class to accomplish the greater goals. At the time, I was teaching this very skill in our government section of fourth grade social studies. I suggested the Board stop their ridiculous waste of time and just choose someone else!

Against the rules of school board meetings, the observers burst into applause when I finished. The next day, the two previous deadlocked candidates stepped aside. Another member was chosen to lead the meetings. Sometimes you have to step up and tell the adults in leadership roles to grow up and act like fourth graders! Be brave. Your knees may shake like mine did, but a profusion of good may come from your message.

Like cogs in a wheel, artistic expressions gloriously spin throughout my community.

FLOWER COGS

Like cogs in a wheel, artistic expressions gloriously spin throughout my community.

After I drew this, it reminded me of an exterior art piece created by my dear friend, Sharon Ohmberger. The clay designs decorate the Burkholder Project's alley wall. This old Haymarket District has become the heart and soul of Lincoln. During nice weather, The Mill is bustling with friendship, conversation and coffee. Cheers for the University of Nebraska team echo down the streets in the fall. A world class wine cellar with the best Indian food is served at The Oven. About five months of Saturdays tout the best farmers market ever! The Amish ladies sell their noodles. Fresh seasonal produce and artistic wares are for sale. These are the anchors that serve as the cogged wheels of my community.

What varied arts spin and bring your community together? Supporting and participating in the arts or gatherings makes you a cog in the wheel of belonging.

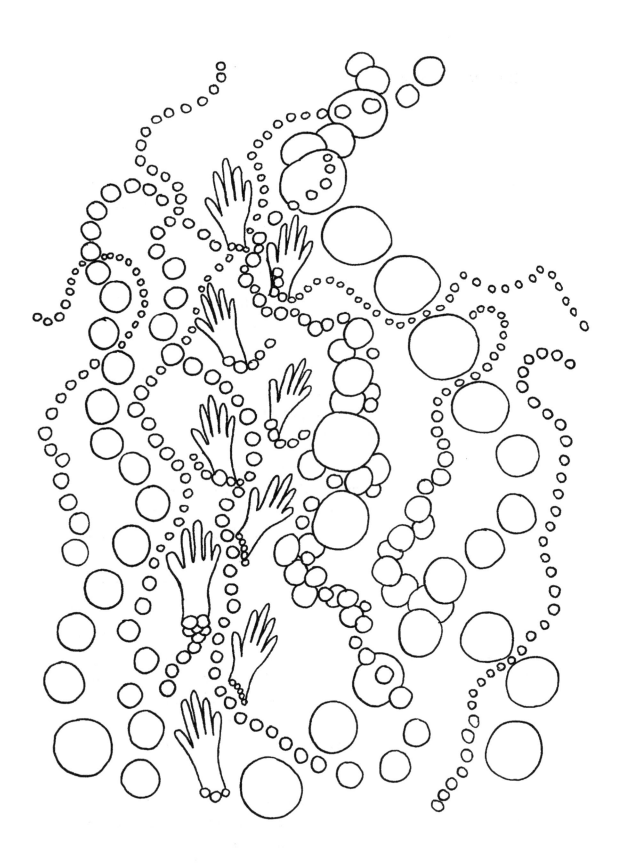

Honest, helpful, caring people always arrive at the perfect time to assist me.

HELPING HANDS

Honest, helpful, caring people always arrive at the perfect time to assist me.

I don't understand why people are reluctant to ask for help. Most folks I know are more than happy to assist friends, even strangers, if they can. I want to encourage you to ask for help when you need it by telling you my story.

When George H. W. Bush was President, the military was drastically downsized. We went from being a Navy family to jobless, debt-free people returning to their favorite place they'd ever been stationed. With $20,000 we bought the dumpiest house in Lincoln's Near South Neighborhood. I took a sledgehammer to a wall ten minutes after closing. Rob heroically pulled out the animal-urinated carpet. Our kindergartener and fourth grader had their own goggles and tools of destruction too. We filled a wheat truck five times with trash and debris from this neglected 1½ story bungalow. We had a need, muscle, hope, and a learning curve.

After months of work, October arrived, and we weren't to the point of being able to move in. Having previously belonged to the Near South Neighborhood Association, we had immediately joined again. I knew there were people who loved saving old homes. I called every single member asking them if they would kindly lend a hand for any amount of time or contribute drinks or snacks to the work crew. I only knew a handful of those I called.

On the designated weekend, I nailed a big sheet of paper on the front door listing all of the tasks we needed to have accomplished. As people arrived, I thanked them and told them to choose anything they enjoyed doing. "I came because I couldn't believe your tenacity. I wanted to see this," declared one woman. An elderly couple brought apple juice and watched for a while. Did you know some people enjoy scraping paint? It was an amazing gathering of helpful people that gathered in our bubble – most of whom didn't even know us!

Just before the end of October, we got the dry wall up and moved in. I wrote each and every helper a thank you note. Over 130 people ended up assisting or touring our house through the seven years it took to finish it. Every helping hand along the way gave their gifts to us willingly. Please know that if you ask, you will likely receive. Color these hands helpful and willing!

Relationships founded on kindness, respect and love,
greatly enrich my heart and soul.

OPEN HEART

Relationships founded on kindness, respect and love,
greatly enrich my heart and soul.

Once I was the one shoveling snow for an elderly neighbor. Now I am the recipient of this kindness. When a child, I addressed my friends' parents as Mr. or Mrs., and now I'm Ms. Ropes. Luckily, I had very loving extended family members. Later, loving friends. Then I innately learned what it was like to love as a parent, that "I'll lay my life down in exchange for yours anytime" kind of love.

When acts of kindness, signs of respect, and love are present in my day, my soul sparkles. Show others you care today and see if you don't have a happy heart before you go to sleep tonight.

Those I call family flock together to nurture, support, and experience joy.

TRUSTERO FAMILY BIRDS

Those I call family flock together to nurture, support, and experience joy.

My grandmother's trustero is a beautiful cabinet that now sits in my home holding special serving dishes and glassware. Carved and painted birds decorate the functional piece of art. Its birds inspired my drawing and affirmation. Special glasses and Nambe serving pieces come out of the trustero when people in my flock gather.

Families can be, and usually are, complicated. I try to love all people knowing they are people too, but some humans I will never understand. This includes some family members. I've learned to release the difficult ones to the Higher Power for understanding and judgement. For my sanity and pleasure, many non-relatives are included in my wonderful family circle. We support and nurture one another as lovingly as we can.

Thankfully, having a "family of choice" is now an accepted societal norm. I am the "fifth kid" in one family where four were birthed. I have a "sister" who was an only child. I have my "hockey boys" and hope they still regard me as their "Mom Unit."

No matter who gave birth to whom, the color of skin, cultural differences, or even if they will likely be a member for a season, celebrate your family! Military families are especially experienced with this kind of family flow. Gather your flock and celebrate absolutely anything. Enjoy!

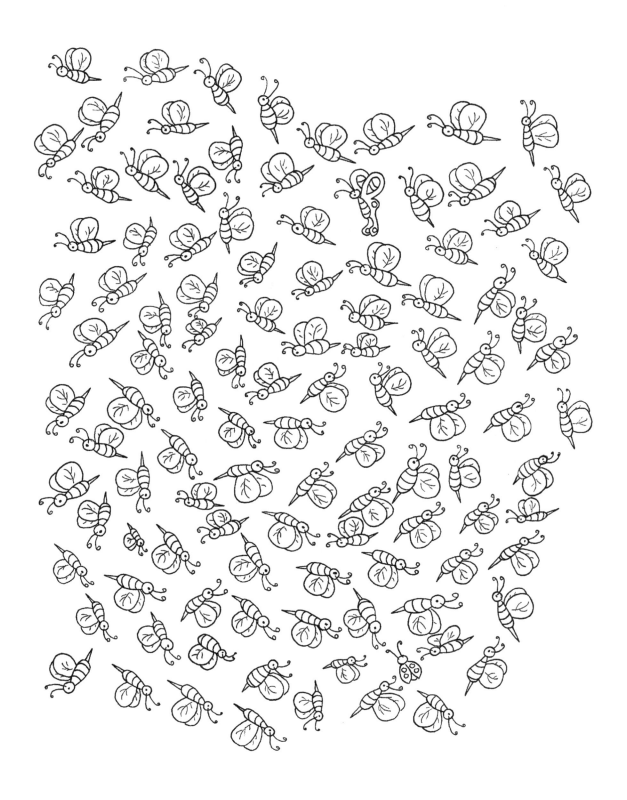

*Positive energy pollinates my subconscious thoughts
and the words that flow from me.*

FLIGHT OF THE BUMBLEBEES

Positive energy pollinates my subconscious thoughts
and the words that flow from me.

While living in Bozeman, Montana, my great-grandmother, Mabel Hendricks Harvey, taught piano until age 81. From age four to eight, I would often spend the night with her.

I can still easily visualize her playing "Flight of the Bumblebee" whenever I hear the classical piece. She was one of the most positive pollinators of my life.

I've been told by many that she never said an unkind word about anyone. She would read to me from Unity Church's publication, *Daily Word*, a publication I now read daily. In part, I believe her daily practice of reading and speaking kindly reinforced her positive nature as years progressed. Grammy was my early teacher example of the power of positive thought. As an adult, I began studying how to harness this attitude and mindset. My boys have plenty of stories when I wasn't a role model. If you raised kids, you might give me some grace on this point. Sometimes my stinger came out! Just like most skills, practice and reminders, like putting affirmations on mirrors and walls, helped me recover more quickly over time.

Perhaps you will use this page as your reminder. What positive thoughts and statements will you have today?

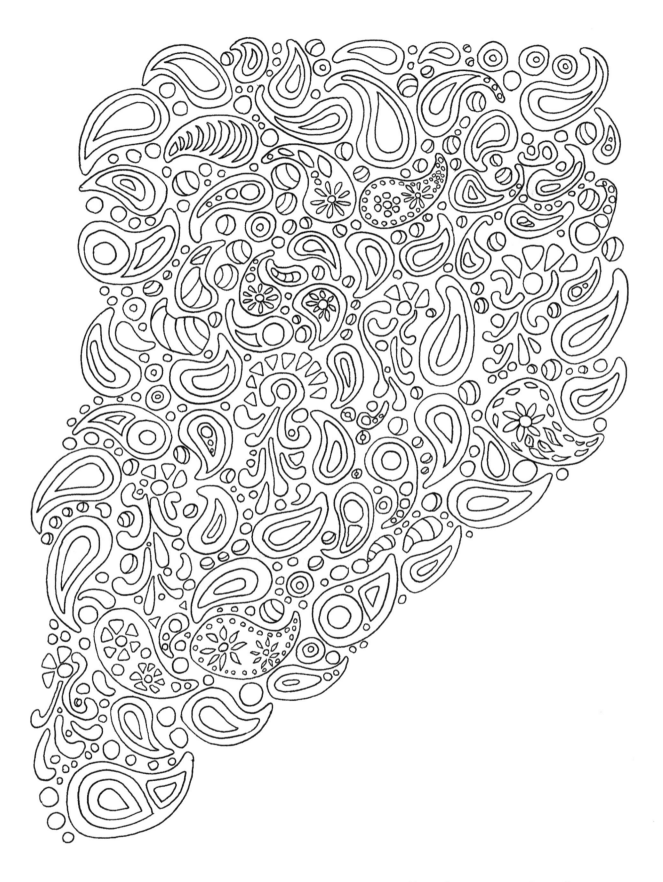

Inspiration comes to me when I take time for myself. Relaxing my thoughts,
I allow Divine Guidance and Direction to expand my spark of insight.

PAISLEY POWER

Inspiration comes to me when I take time for myself. Relaxing my thoughts, I allow Divine Guidance and Direction to expand my spark of insight.

This design was a relaxation process. My mind and hand relaxed. I had no preconceived notion about what I might draw. The first paisley just lead to the next. Spontaneous free forms filled the spaces in between. An initial line became a greater expanding whole. The page came to be.

Trying to solve problems, find misplaced items, or pulling together a creative plan can sometimes feel like pushing the proverbial rock up the endless hill. Many inventors and brilliant thinkers have shared their practice of relaxing, focusing on another task, or even sleeping in order to have a solution come to them. In other words, they opened to Divine Direction.

Relax, be open to color choices just coming to you. Do you need help finding a solution? Relax. I know making room for Divine Guidance will serve you well. Receive your special spark and watch it expand!

*Seeing only part of my future, I walk into it. Remembering to appreciate
the here and now, I affirm the use of my best judgment at each turn.*

Rocky Mountains

Seeing only part of my future, I walk into it. Remembering to appreciate the here and now, I affirm the use of my best judgment at each turn.

Having lived along the Rocky Mountains a good portion of my life, I know surprises are around curves. Stunning wildflowers, rock formations, the beauty of freshly fallen snow, wild animals, even the occasional old, deserted building can be explored. Rarely do I look upon the snowcapped mountains and say, "Why can't they be covered in flowers now?" Obviously, because it is not the season for that view!

Unfortunately, I have had my eye on the future too many times in my life that I did not fully embrace my current season. I'm not alone. Little kids can't wait to get big. Tweens can't wait to become drivers. Students can't wait to graduate. Young parents look forward to sleeping through the night. On we go.

There is a country song where an older man tells the younger to appreciate the circumstances that he is going through because, "You're going to miss this." Looking back, I do wish I had had more appreciation of the here and now. My path has been anything but straight, but it has been interesting. As my grandmother Dussy used to say to me, "Your life is never boring!"

Appreciate today's surroundings, seasons, and loved ones. Then make informed decisions about your future. You'll probably end up on a different mountain top than you were originally hiking toward, but I bet you will love the view!

The art of purposeful placement allows beneficial energy to flow in my favor.

FENG SHUI

The art of purposeful placement allows beneficial energy to flow in my favor.

In the early 1990's, in order to help my friend, Pat, I was asked to read the first book written in English about the ancient Chinese art of Feng Shui. We learned from author Sara Rossbach's book, *Interior Design with Feng Shui,* how to create energetic balance using this ancient art with a twist. Instead of using cardinal directions, as had been the tradition for thousands of years, readers were instructed how to superimpose the octagonal bagua onto a room using its doorway for baseline placement.

The entrance to a room or building will align either in Knowledge and Spirituality to the left, Career in the center, or Helpful People and Travel on the right. These words are along the bottom of your Feng Shui page. Rather than the traditional octagonal bagua that positions the eight life aspects in relation to one another, this one is drawn as a rectangle. It still works! Using the placement of entrances as they relate to a room to superimpose the bagua's aspects onto a floor plan is much easier than trying to reorient a home because it faces north instead of south.

Over a few years, Pat and I became Feng Shui consultants with clients primarily in Nebraska. Here I offer a fun bagua for you to color and use no matter where you live.

Superimposing the attributes around the space, what do you see in each gua? Is your wealth area cluttered like your purse? Is your relationship gua storing a pile of dirty clothes? I hope not! Have fun and know that clearing the clutter and placing representational items purposefully is only part of the process, but an important part.

I ask expectantly, reaching for the Light. I listen.
My purpose is revealed, and I act!

REACHING BLOSSOMS

I ask expectantly, reaching for the Light. I listen.
My purpose is revealed, and I act!

When asked if you are living your purpose, how do you respond? Downheartedly or with an inner glow of knowing you are in your right place? I ask because during a recent sermon about finding purpose, a large number of people were signaling that they didn't know theirs. They had let other people, or their own doubts keep them from exploring their true path. I was luckier.

I am living proof that success may not always look like the obvious, or even a recommended choice. I returned to college as a non-traditional student majoring in Great Plains Studies. "What will you do with that?" was echoed by strangers and people I knew were actually in my corner. I didn't know what I would do with the degree. I just knew I was passionate about my studies and felt like the luckiest student on campus. My mother thought they made the major just for me. Exactly!

I was the fourth person to graduate with this unique degree. My passion became part of my profession thereafter. Sometimes my knowledge was the foundation of the job. At other times it was a helpful addendum. The important lesson is that it may not look like I've had a successful, monied career by normal American standards, but I have had joy and passion in my work.

My purpose was revealed in an obscure major in a town we lived in just long enough for me to complete my studies before we were transferred. My purpose was revealed, and I acted. You can too!

Like a cactus flower, the prickly people around me have a
delicate bloom within. I concentrate on that fragile beauty.

CACTUS FLOWER

Like a cactus flower, the prickly people around me have a
delicate bloom within. I concentrate on that fragile beauty.

Thick skin and fine sharp needles protect tough cactus from the harsh Tucson
climate. This large cactus grows in Ashlie's backyard outside the guestroom
door. During my visit, it captured more of my attention than usual,
because it was in bloom.

New green leaf pods clustered along the tops of the cladodes. Those yet to
open had moist looking raspberry-colored buds. Their symmetrical positions
pointed to the upper cluster of thickly packed crimson protectors. When the
incredibly delicate flowers opened, the surprise was the petals
were nearly translucent orange.

The opportunity for pollination is small by comparison to flowers of the
Midwest. Robust for only one day, wilting begins the next. Shortly after the
petals fall away, a smooth-looking hollow of the barest honeydew melon
green appears. I ran my finger inside to discover minute spines
poking my skin.

I've known prickly people from whom I initially wanted to run away. Hard
to work with, their tough exteriors and verbal barbs purposefully kept people
away. They probably got that way from the eco-system in which they were
raised. However, given a few seasons, they usually ended up revealing a
beautiful moment now and then.

Smartly, don't get stuck by a barb, but let's concentrate on the
hidden beauty within the prickly people in our lives.

I invite kindred spirits to walk with me sharing conversations and quiet times.

KINDRED SPIRIT

I invite kindred spirits to walk with me sharing conversations and quiet times.

This drawing incorporates two of my favorite spirits – my dog's and the spirit of the land at my sister and brother-in-law's home. Whether being with my sister sharing conversations, walking with my dog and enjoying her comforting presence, or just walking across their bridge and sitting, admiring the energy of the creek and land, I feel as though I am with a kindred spirit.

We all need those kindred spirits with whom we can let loose and laugh from the center of our beings. Who is the friend that really listens to you and with whom you share sincere conversations? Where do you go to feel at peace and just hear the quiet whispers from Spirit or to just be? Invite one of your kindred spirits to join you today. Celebrate your togetherness!

I work through each challenge knowing it is part of my metamorphosis.

METAMORPHOSIS

I work through each challenge knowing it is part of my metamorphosis.

The caterpillar retreats to remake itself into a butterfly. This metamorphosis is easy to see and follow within two weeks. Human stages are easy to qualify until defining the adult chapter. This last stage has a large age variation according to countries, religious traditions, or family situations. Most in my generation couldn't wait to get their first apartments and decorate them with scrounged up, borrowed or repurposed boards. Today, minimalist stylin' kids wouldn't dream of taking that old couch from the family room!

Beyond physical, most of us have markers in our lives that changed us tremendously. We move through schooling to first careers. Family status changes. Events in countries change us. The United States went from the "Camelot" phase to shock when President John F. Kennedy was assassinated. September 11, 2001 plummeted the world into mourning when planes were overtaken and rerouted for terror, shattering thousands of lives in the World Trade Center, the Pentagon, and in a Pennsylvania field.

Positively, the Olympics, space exploration, the Berlin Wall falling, the music of Yo-Yo Ma, the care envisioned by Mother Theresa, and many more people and events have had the power to lift up groups, countries, continents, and even the world's consciousness.

No doubt, on a very personal level, we have all had our challenges that have changed us. Some of us need more help to focus on the possibilities in front of us rather than the event that caused the change. May you have the perseverance and support to see your challenges as an opportunity to spread your beautiful wings and fly!

A fanciful day awaits me. A door opens to a creative solution.

Hidden Fairy Farm

A fanciful day awaits me. A door opens to a creative solution.

When a girl, I would build tiny towns for my playmates to fulfill their needs. Imaginary to others, but as real to me as my parents, the sprites and fairies were happy to live with my creations. Where might we, as adults with creative minds and talents, find a fanciful outlet today? I think of the web sites dedicated to creative solutions and the willingness to share. Adapting others' creativity to meet your own needs saves time and gives a springboard to your imaginative results.

Whether fulfilling a need to reorganize, sew, paint, fix, mend, modify, or carve out personal time, open that door to a creative solution that fits your fancy!

My friends are a joy to behold! We shine in each others' presence.

R H Ropes

FRIENDSHIP GARDEN

My friends are a joy to behold! We shine in each others' presence.

These plants and flowers are as varied as my circle of friends. We range in socio-economic status, occupations, age, cultures, and the locations where circumstances brought us together. In fact, when compared, many of my friendships only have joy as a common denominator. Orbs and forms of joy include Navy life to Nebraska, from schoolgirl days to teaching school, Bible study to studying metaphysics. Each of my friends brings a bit of a shared past with them when we connect.

Taking care of these friendships is like nurturing a garden. Some are so hearty that it doesn't matter if life hasn't given us the opportunity to see each other in years. We know the runners can be followed to the new node where it still flourishes. Some of us connect but once a year, the brief amaryllis given at Christmastime. Others, a team, might only last a meaningful season. Color your friends connected by joyful sparks!

Only positive and inspirational symbols surround me because I see and feel even when I'm not consciously looking.

Southwest Symbols

*Only positive and inspirational symbols surround me
because I see and feel even when I'm not consciously looking.*

As a Feng Shui consultant, I became very aware of the impact symbols and messages have on our energy fields. Have you ever walked into a room and immediately wanted to turn around and leave? Conversely, have you ever entered a space and thought you would love the opportunity to stay for hours? Rooms and the things within have an effect on us.

You are not obligated to have something in your space if it doesn't work for you; even if it came from a well-meaning relative. As my sister says, "No one gets to decorate my house but me." If it doesn't resonate, regift it! If a sad memory is attached to an item say, "Hasta la vista!" to that thing. Sometimes I see T-shirts and bumper stickers with hurtful statements. What are people thinking by displaying these messages?

Look closely at the magnets on your refrigerator, items on coffee tables and in tucked behind places on shelves. Look at the art on your walls. What messages do they hold for you? If items in your surroundings aren't serving you in a joyful, positive way, get rid of them! Make room for a replacement that is a better fit. Set your intention for a pleasing, positive solution. It will likely come to you in an interesting way and sooner than you think. I've actually made a game of release and replace. I ask myself, "I wonder what will show up for me that is better than I could have imagined?"

Our subconscious minds are marvelous wonders that register hidden meanings and messages. Have your environment energetically work for your higher good by surrounding yourself with positive, inspirational symbols and messages that resonate with you. Want to play release and replace?

Whether physically or through my mind, I relax and experience the environment where I hear Spirit's guidance.

HIDDEN DEER

Whether physically or through my mind, I relax
and experience the environment where I hear Spirit's guidance.

During times when I am seeking a connection to God, sometimes I am able to go to the Rocky Mountains and sit quietly. On several occasions while gazing upon nature, relaxing my mind, praying and welcoming insight, deer have come out of hiding and walked and stood very close to me. Once at the YMCA of the Rockies in Estes Park, I was nearly nose-to-nose with a curious one! During these encounters, I feel my presence has been acknowledged by God and Earth simultaneously.

When I am physically hundreds of miles away from a special spiritual place, but feel the need, I recall the images and embrace the feelings a spiritual encounter invoked. Many of us have been taught techniques to recall a special place in meditation or prayer practices. Visualize the place. Remember the sounds. Recall the smells. Reconnect.

May you remember a special place where you have found peace and go there when you need to. If you don't have that place yet, search. You will find it.

I give myself flowers because I deserve beauty – deep, natural beauty.
Beauty that spills over and out. Beauty that reflects life and me.

BOUQUET

I give myself flowers because I deserve beauty – deep, natural beauty.
Beauty that spills over and out. Beauty that reflects life and me.

When living in Germany and going to the market for food, I noticed how many people walked around with lovely bouquets of flowers. I, too, began purchasing paper-wrapped bunches just for the joy they brought to our tiny one-bedroom apartment.

In America, we tend to send cards and give flowers on holidays that commercialism has abducted. I believe that every day of life is a celebration that warrants beauty. Real beauty! Not the "Barbie" beauty of perfect arrangement. Real flowers we arrange at home. Real beauty of gut-busting laughter. Real food without chemical additives. The sweetness of dirt under the fingernails, of girls and boys making roads for their cars and trucks. Real sweat because there was a frenzied tetherball game in the driveway. The beauty from the heart in a child's piece of art. Laugh lines around eyes. Real beauty in the face and soul of the octogenarian.

Give yourself some real-life beauty. Appreciate yours.

My wealth is represented in many forms. I relax knowing all my needs are met.

NAMBE BOWLS

My wealth is represented in many forms. I relax knowing all my needs are met.

When Feng Shui practitioners ask a person adjusting their surroundings to choose something that represents wealth, it is surprising to me the variety of physical objects clients choose. Your interpretation of your wealth can be as unique as you are. My Nambe bowls not only represent beauty and abundance to me, they are also linked to loving family dinner memories.

Your wealth symbol may be a family heirloom. Perhaps it is something for which you worked very hard so you could buy it. I've seen an item I've regarded as ugly, but was told of the tremendous loving, wealthy memories it contained. Wealth is represented in many forms. It certainly isn't all represented in monetary form.

No matter how you measure your wealth, may all your basic needs be easily met so that there is room for other signs of abundance around you.

Energy flows. Surging vitality courses through the Universe. I tap in.

HYDRANGEA LEAVES

Energy flows. Surging vitality courses through the Universe. I tap in.

A high school friend took a photo of these hydrangea leaves. The image captivated me. I saw the paths of life-giving energy so clearly.

We can see the effects of energy reacting in a myriad of ways in our world. Rushing water, bending grasses, spinning turbines, even running children, give us visual evidence of the existence of great kinetic power. To my knowledge, we cannot see energy as an entity. We know it exists. We can feel it warming our skin or esoterically, warming our hearts. We use positive thought energy to great effect in our lives. We use prayer energy for healing over great distances. We call it God energy, laws of physics, Universal Power.

Through veins in leaves, we can examine the course through which nourishment is delivered. Envision the paths that bring you energy. From your physical being to your mental thought waves. Tap in. It is yours for the taking.

Like the gift of unconditional love from a best friend, I accept the gift of philautia, the unconditional love of compassion and forgiveness for myself. I affirm I am a child of God working to be better each day.

Agape Blossoms

*Like the gift of unconditional love from a best friend, I accept the gift of philautia,
the unconditional love of compassion and forgiveness for myself.
I affirm I am a child of God working to be better each day.*

This is one of my favorite drawings because it incorporates a being who loves me unconditionally. Sending that level of love to those we like is much easier than attempting to love someone we oppose. It is a big job for most of us. I believe that most of the religions of the world have stories that teach how we should love one another. No doubt we strive for this, but what about loving ourselves?

There have been days when I haven't approved of how a person acted but still loved them. Sometimes we need to give the grace to ourselves as we would to our best friend, our lover, our child. There are days when I certainly have not loved myself because of my own actions. Having been mis-aligned I have to re-align myself with my Higher Power and in my heart.

If you need to re-align, make room for compassion and forgiveness for yourself. Give yourself a good dose of philautia. Know that you are a human child of God. Tomorrow is a new beginning, a day to do better.

CPSIA information can be obtained
at www.ICGtesting.com
Printed in the USA
LVHW050339070621
689537LV00009B/217